T0209692

ADRIANA'S STORY

FINDING HOPE

ADRIANA J

BALBOA.PRESS

A DIVISION OF HAY HOUSE

Balboa Press books may be ordered through booksellers or by contacting:

Balboa Press
A Division of Hay House
1663 Liberty Drive
Bloomington, IN 47403
www.balboapress.com
844-682-1282

Print information available on the last page.

ISBN: 979-8-7652-4546-0 (sc)
ISBN: 979-8-7652-4547-7 (hc)
ISBN: 979-8-7652-4545-3 (e)

Library of Congress Control Number: 2023918608

Balboa Press rev. date: 11/17/2023

REVIEWS

"This poignant story captures your heart. My modest upbringing seems regal, compared to the hardship Adriana endured"

- Donna Lucreziano

"When I first met Adriana, I remember thinking, what a strong, amazing woman she is…a true determined single mom at the time, building a future for herself and her family. She had dreams and fulfilled it. I am truly inspired by her life story.

Honestly…her story inspired me to do better in life. I honor her as a woman and beautiful life built in spite of all her challenges she had endured."

- Maria Vaduva

This book is dedicated to
my children Athena & Jennifer, and to Susie in heaven;
my grandchildren Nico, Oliver, Rocco,
Jordanna and Serenna,
who give me hope, joy, and inspiration;
and to Arek - my ride or die; my
partner in life; and the one
who brings me happiness, encouragement,
laughter, and adventures.

CONTENTS

ACKNOWLEDGEMENTS

My friends and family, and even strangers, have encouraged me to write my story, and I am thankful to them. I would like to especially thank Arek and my long-time friend Donna, for their unending love and support. And also, I would like to thank Connie, who passed away recently, for her many years of friendship and encouragement. And lastly, a heartfelt thank you to my wonderful editor and friend Juliet Sullivan.

Note from author

This book portrays the harsh images of my life. I'm writing about these dark and challenging times because, like everyone, I have spent my life searching for hope, a better life, and happiness. One of the reasons I am happy to share my book is to capture this simple and beautiful message: positive thoughts work. During the hard times it's very difficult to remain positive, and I have battled with this challenge daily, but when I work to give out good energy; to be kind in the face of anger and fear; to help whenever I can; and to attract a happy life by choosing to look for it, it really does change my day. Whether in the past or present, whenever I encounter hard obstacles, I try the same approach: to stay positive.

If you have chosen to read this book, I would like to thank you for giving me a chance to tell you my story.

My life growing up was very different than my children's. Not only have times changed, but my earlier years took place on a different continent, with a different culture and traditions. It was, and is, important to me that my children and grandchildren know and understand my history and its impact on my life.

I believe that everyone has a story. This is mine.

INTRODUCTION

Nicolette

Outside the air was crisp and the sun was shining, but inside the streetcar the air was stale and stuffy. Sitting squeezed between two strangers, Nicolette held her newborn baby tightly to her chest.

There was a thick mixture of odours which seemed to cling to her skin; from the sour smell of sweat from the man sitting on one side of her, to the cloyingly sweet perfume from the woman on the other. Nicolette felt anxious and fearful. Becoming a new mother was overwhelming.

She was on her way home from the hospital, where she had given birth to a baby girl just a few days earlier. After a long and strenuous labour, she felt tired and worried, not knowing what the future would hold.

This is the very first picture of me (Age one)

She wanted to protect her baby but didn't know how. Waves of different thoughts raced through her mind.

How would she manage to take care of this tiny baby girl? Nicolette didn't have anything material to give her daughter. All she could offer her was love. As the streetcar rumbled along, she gazed at the sweet, sleeping face of the little being nestling in her arms, and realized that her feelings were jumbled; she wasn't sure what she felt.

She was proud and happy that she had actually produced such a beautiful human being; a feeling of pure love washed through her. She wanted to give her daughter the best care she could, and to protect her from everyone and everything. But at the same time, she felt overwhelmed, uncertain and sad.

Was it possible to give her daughter everything she herself never had? The thought of failing her daughter filled Nicolette with fear. The responsibility of raising a child bore down on her heavily, and she knew that she would be doing it alone.

Nicolette lived in Bucharest, Romania, which was a poor, dictator-led communist country. Life was hard enough, but to raise a child as a single mother in the mid-fifties, in a country where a communist regime and poverty dominated, was a formidable prospect.

She hadn't yet felt able to tell her mother that the baby's father, her husband Paul, had run out on her while she was pregnant

Much to her surprise, Paul had unexpectedly arrived at the hospital the day the baby was born. He had walked into the ward, peered into the crib where his tiny daughter was sleeping, and without speaking, walked out again. He did not come back; and Nicolette would never see him again.

She never knew why he came that day, but any hope she had that he would somehow be a father to their baby was soon replaced by a realization that he had chosen not be a part of their lives. He clearly felt no responsibility or obligation towards his daughter, and never would.

Nicolette was a beautiful woman, with long, brown, wavy hair; deep brown eyes and a voluptuous, curvy body. She was also deaf and mute, but she didn't mind. She was born like that and didn't know any other way.

Shortly after they arrived home from the hospital, both baby and mother became gravely ill. Family and friends urged Nicolette to get the baby baptized as soon as possible, so her baby could go to heaven in case the unthinkable happened (this was a Romanian belief). Another Romanian tradition was that the baby should be named after one of their godparents. Nicolette named her baby girl "Adriana", after her godmother. The godparents were close friends and a kind couple who loved children but never had any of their own. Adriana was their tenth godchild.

After the baptism, everyone who had seen how sick the baby had been said a miracle had happened: Adriana got well.

By the time she was six months old, Adriana was a healthy, chubby and happy baby, although unaware of the hardship that life would bring. That baby was me.

Outside our front door (Age three)

CHAPTER ONE

ROMANIA: THE EARLY YEARS

My mom told me that when I was six months old, I somehow sensed that she could not hear me cry, so I would motion and even grab and tug her arm whenever I was hungry. As well, if someone was knocking on the door, I would point to it. By the time I was three years old, I could communicate by sign language perfectly and I became my mother's little helper. Later, I realized that even from the beginning, I was fighting for survival.

From that time on, I would go everywhere with my mother - to the doctor's office, the grocery store, her workplace; anywhere she needed me to interpret for her. I didn't just help my mother out, but also her deaf and mute friends, who were isolated because of their disability.

My life revolved around my mother and her friends as I went with them anywhere they needed help with communicating.

My mother cherished and took good care of me. She used to say, "You are my ears, mouth and heart. You are my everything."

For the first five years of my life, we lived in a one-room house with a small courtyard in the centre of Bucharest. There was no ventilation, and no bathroom or kitchen, although there was an outhouse in the backyard. In one corner of the room was a stand with a two-burner gas stove on it. We did not have an oven or a refrigerator.

I remember it being cold and dark, and I can still recall the pangs of hunger I felt in those early years.

A picture of me and a caring neighbour at Christmas time, in the room where we lived (Age four)

My mother's younger sister, Petra, lived with us. Petra was also deaf and mute. She and my mother slept in the same bed and I slept in a crib next to their bed. When I got out of my crib, I had to jump onto their bed and then jump again onto the floor. The room had only one door, four feet from the bed, which led outside.

A single 40-watt light bulb hung from the ceiling and this light would blink when the doorbell rang to alert my mother and aunt that someone was at the door.

My Aunt Petra loved me very much. Whenever she could, she would take me to the park or for a visit with her friends to show me off. When we were on our outings, strangers often thought that I was her little girl. My aunt once told me that she loved the fact that I never gave the truth away; that I was not her daughter but her niece.

My mother was protective of her younger sister; she did not want her going out with boys, especially not if I was with her.

Aunt Petra and I were very close and she played a big part in my life. She knew how to make me feel good, no matter how hard the times were. She was loving, fun and generous. From time to time she would do special things for me; I remember her taking me to the park and buying me candy, which was such a treat. Although her loving gestures may seem trivial by today's standards, they had a huge impact on me.

One of my most cherished memories of Aunt Petra was when I was about four years old and returned from a summer camp. The camp was sponsored by the factory where my mother worked, and was organized for poor and under-privileged children of their workers.

The summer camp was held in the beautiful Carpathian Mountains which run through Romania. I remember this time as being a wonderfully happy three weeks, although I never again had a chance to go back, as the factory only offered it that one time.

When I arrived back in the city after camp, I saw Aunt Petra waiting for me at the bus stop. I felt like my heart would explode when I saw her standing there, holding a doll for me. This was my first doll and the only one I would have for a very long time (maybe this explains why I now love to collect dolls).

My mom and aunt did not have an easy childhood. My grandfather died when my mother was three years old. Even though my mother was so young when her father died, she remembered him because of the loving things he did for her and her sister. They were poor in those days (though not as poor as they were later when dictator Nicolae Ceausescu came into power), but despite this, my mother remembered her father taking her and her sister to fun fairs and to markets.

Aunt Petra and me.

The story my mother told about her father's death, passed on to her from her mother, was that one day he went to lay in bed with excruciating stomach pains and simply died there. Later on, I learned that his death was probably caused by a burst appendix. Little was known of appendicitis at the time, and there were no doctors nearby to treat him.

My grandmother was sweet, witty and softly-spoken, with a big heart. She lived in a small rural village twenty kilometers from Bucharest. After my grandfather died in his thirties, she was left to raise two daughters and a son by herself, although she never complained.

My mother's younger brother was not deaf and mute. Later on, when he was supposed to go to the army (which was mandatory in Romania), my grandmother begged the authorities to let him stay home, as she was a single mother and she needed his help. They agreed, but this turned out to be a mistake as he became verbally abusive to my grandmother and his sisters.

I once asked my grandmother why both her girls were born deaf and mute. She told me: "When I was pregnant with Nicolette, I met a deaf and mute pregnant lady," as if that was an explanation. After conducting my own research, I feel it was more likely caused by my grandmother having contracted German measles while pregnant.

At that time, children in Romania started school when they were seven years old. My grandmother decided to send her two girls to the only school in the country for deaf and mute children.

The school was in Timisoara, a city located some 500 kilometers away from their home. It broke my grandmother's heart for her girls to be so far away, but this was the only way they would get their basic education. My grandmother never had the chance to get an education, so she made sure her children did.

My grandmother was able to visit her girls just once a year, and she couldn't afford to bring them home for Christmas, Easter or summer holidays. My mother once told me how hard it was for her and her sister to see the other children go home for holidays. To earn her upkeep and take her mind off being left behind, my mother would use the time she had to clean the school, starting with the kitchen, including the dishes and utensils.

When she finished with the kitchen, my mother moved on to the large bedrooms which had around 20 beds to a room.

My mom's schoolmate and best friend Valentina later told me that she would only eat with the utensils that her friend - my mother - had cleaned. She only trusted the cleanliness of the tableware Mom had washed because she was obsessed with detail, sanitation and organization.

My mother recalled how one day during the war, the bombs started to rain down all around them, so the teacher gathered the children together and hurried them into the school's basement, where they were told to stay quiet. The children could feel the closeness of the explosions and were terribly frightened. My mother said her heart was beating so hard it felt like it was going to come out of her chest.

When she was around fifteen or sixteen, she developed tuberculosis in her eyes, which completely blinded her. Soon after my mother was diagnosed, the schoolmaster called a meeting with all of the teachers and the principal.

At this meeting, he proposed taking my mother's life by shooting her. His reason, he explained, was that with her being deaf, mute, and now blind, she would be of no use to society. He further suggested that they could take advantage of the war by using it as a cover for the shooting, so no-one would know they were responsible for my mother's death. Fortunately, the principal disagreed and the idea was eliminated altogether. The principal saved her life and my mother always remembered him fondly for that, though she carried a deep emotional scar with her from this memory.

When my mother finished grade eleven, Aunt Petra, who was two years younger, did not want to stay at the school without her sister, and so both girls left the school and went home to their mother.

My grandmother took my mother to a doctor in the city to treat her eyes. Every day for thirty days, they made the day-long bus trip into Bucharest, where the doctor injected medicine into my mother's eyes. She said it was the most painful experience that she had endured in her life. After a month of the injections, she was thankful as her eyesight progressively improved.

Once she had recovered, my mother started to look for work, and at twenty, she moved to Bucharest with Petra, where she got a job in a factory as a sewing machine operator. This was the only job she ever held.

CHAPTER TWO

MEMORIES OF ROMANIA

Romania is located in the southeastern part of Central Europe and is famous for the region of Transylvania, where Bran Castle, the gothic home to the legendary Count Dracula, nestles in the rugged Carpathian Mountains.

Today, Romania has a fast-developing, diverse economy with growing upper and middle classes. The expansive, sandy beaches lining the Black Sea; impressive medieval castles; and charming, historic villages and cities have made it a popular destination for domestic and foreign visitors.

However, in the sixties and seventies, when I grew up there, the country - with a population of around 20 million - was under communist rule and strained by widespread poverty. Everything was owned by the government; no private businesses existed. From 1974, the communist party was led by Nicolae Ceausescu, whose practice was to export everything – including clothing and food - to other countries, while its own people were deprived of the very things they were making or growing with their own hands.

The government also owned all of the farms. In return for their hard work, farmers received a set amount of food from the government, but it wasn't nearly enough for a family to survive on.

Work was mandatory and everyone over the age of sixteen (if not going to school) had to have a job. You might be wondering how the authorities could find out who did not have a job. The police could stop anybody, anywhere, for any or no reason, and since our photo IDs had to be dated and stamped with our address of residence as well as our place of work, it was easy to find out what a person's work status was.

After I finished high school, I was trying to decide what I should do - look for a summer job, or continue my education in the fall, if I could leave the country. The government was checking who was registered as working and who was not. I was one of many young people who they found not to be working. We were all given notice, and then had to get on a truck which took us to an unknown place outside the city. They dropped us at a muddy field, where we were instructed to pull potatoes from the ground and sort them into crates.

We were not paid for this arduous work; we were just given some coupons for food. This was meant as punishment.

In the cities, factories were housed in giant buildings and most people made minimum wage (again, not enough to feed a family). On the main floor of the factories, the government provided day care for the workers' children. This was one of the few things that the communist system offered its people.

Although the government was constructing many new residential apartment buildings, the chance of the average Romanian getting a unit was slim. There was a waiting list of about ten years. To get on the list, factory workers had to sign up with the office where they worked. Because the government owned the buildings, the allocation of the units was controlled by them.

Apartment buildings were considered a luxury at the time because they had central heating and a bathroom with everything a bathroom had in a modern world. People like us, who did not have a bathroom in their home, would go to a place called "the bathhouse," located in the city centre, which had rows and rows of shower stalls.

When I was three years old, I went with my mother to her factory's office to help interpret; we were putting our names on the waiting list for an apartment. I had been to the office many times, so the ladies knew me there.

I remember in particular a lady by the name of Anna Maria who was always cheerful and happy to see me. She would pick me up and would sit me on her desk. All the other office ladies then would circle her desk. They would comment on how cute I was, and then they would admire my clothes, commenting on how my mother made sure our clothes were always clean. (My mother used to dress me in crisp, white clothes to go to the office.) Anna Maria would say, "Nicolette is poor, but very clean. Look at the spotless clothes little Adriana is wearing." Everyone we met used to say this about us.

Each lady would bring me something; an apple, some chocolate or other snacks. After that, they would wait patiently for me to start interpreting what my mother was saying to me in sign language. Because I was little, my "translation" would be child-like; my words coming out exactly as a child would speak. This time it went like this: "Please let us live in an apartment with a kitchen and a bathroom. We live in one small room and my mom has to put the potatoes and onions under the bed. It smells and I am little and is not good for me." The ladies were charmed, I suppose, as our names went on the priority list.

They told us to make sure to stop by every month to chat and to find out when we would get the apartment. We did visit every month, and by the time I was five years old, just two years after my mother had applied, we were told that a new one-bedroom apartment – with its own bathroom! - was available for us. I can still remember the excitement and joy of that day.

In early March there were flowers coming out of the ground. On Women's Day (March 8), boys and men would give flowers to girls and women. There was a tradition in Romania where boys gave out trinkets, pinning them to the girls' clothes, like broaches. This is the only time from my childhood (there were very few) that I enjoyed and fondly remember. At school it was like a friendly competition between the girls (which one of us had the most trinkets pinned on their chest). The trinket in the Romanian language is called "martisor."

Life in Romania was tough, and being the daughter of a deaf and mute single mother made life even tougher.

I have a memory of standing at a crosswalk, holding my mom's hand and waiting for the light to turn green so we could cross. An older, grey-haired man shuffled up beside us and pleaded, "Can you spare some change, so I can buy a piece of bread? I just got out of jail and have no-one."

I felt so sad for the man. I tugged at my mom's arm, trying to convey what he had said. My mom was watching the light intently. The man repeated his request, a note of desperation creeping into his voice. My eyes teared up with sadness, and frustration that I could not make my mother understand. I held my mother's hand tighter as we crossed the street. I started to cry, but my sobs were unheard. "What's wrong?" Mom finally mouthed to me. But it was too late. The man had disappeared.

Our standard of living was very different from that of our Canadian counterparts in the seventies and eighties. Home telephones were a luxury reserved for high-ranking officials. Transportation between countries was impossibly expensive, and travelling by air was unthinkable. So we had to resort to writing letters in order to keep in touch with anyone outside our area.

For decades, the opportunity to move abroad was mostly reserved for those who had influential ties or had family living abroad. It was an extreme rarity for a normal citizen to be able to move away.

From an early age I knew I wanted to leave Romania. From my teenage years onwards, I spent much of my time reaching for what seemed like an impossible dream; but something was driving me forward and I never gave up. I had a small group of friends, and together we made a plan of how to get away, where to go and where to get help once we got to one of the Western countries.

Despite every obstacle written into my life history; in spite of my poor, humble upbringing and the constant hardships I faced along the way, I was eventually to realize my teenage dream.

CHAPTER THREE

SURVIVAL

The factory organized Christmas parties for the workers' children. Parents were asked what their child or children needed, so Santa could get it for them. Every three years parents could ask for large presents.

When it was time to ask for a bigger gift, my mom would always ask for a coat for me. I was growing fast and in those three years, my winter coat would be getting too small. Because my coat sleeves were too short, I was hiding my arms behind my back in public and especially at school. Every time I received a coat from Santa, I was as happy as kids are now when they receive their favourite toys, computers, or phones. I appreciated it with all my heart and in return, I wanted to help those around me.

My mother's income was low, so there was never enough money to buy the food we needed. Later on, my neighbours told me how my mom would skip meals, and in the winter she would wear a thin jacket and sandals, just to make sure I would not go hungry and was always warm.

Since I can remember, there was a shortage of all things people needed to survive. Food, furniture, appliances; even jewellery such as wedding rings, were hard to find.

Whenever people needed anything at all, they would get up early in the morning and line up outside the store. Most of the time they did not know what they would get. For example, in a butcher shop, no one knew if they would get chicken, beef or pork, but it did not matter; they were happy to get any kind of meat.

Sometimes, people would go back home empty handed, either because the truck food did not arrive that day or because by the time people finally got to the counter there was no meat left. It was the same with everything else; any other groceries, clothes, furniture; the necessities of life. In the 1980s the economic situation and poverty got so bad that the government put a cap on the quantity of food that could be bought. For instance, in the bigger cities, for a family of four, food was rationed to 3kg of meat, six litres of milk, 13kg of vegetables, and 1kg each of oil and sugar; all per month.*

* This rationing – deemed to be one of the most drastic austerity measures in peacetime - was introduced by Ceausescu in an attempt to pay off the country's national debt. Coupled with electricity and heating shortages as well as severe repercussions for any sort of political dissent, the Romanian people suffered years of extreme humiliation, poverty and malnutrition.

When we moved into the new apartment, we needed appliances, such as a stove and fridge. In order for us to get these, we had to get organized and get up every morning at 5 a.m. to hop on the streetcar, and then a bus, so we could be the first in line at the appliance store. I remember how worried I felt, thinking that we might not get the appliances. I was only five years old and I was worried about these grown-up things, but times were tough and the reality is that is all I had known since I could remember: poverty and struggling for life's necessities.

It took three weeks until we were finally able to buy the appliances. I remember the anxiety and stress we went through to make sure we got the things we needed for the new apartment. At the same time, we were excited and happy to have a place of our own. The fresh, new white paint in the apartment seemed to transport us into a different era. I felt like floating in the air with happiness. Having basic things meant so much to us.

Unfortunately, by the time I was seven years old, my mother became increasingly ill. I remember going to different doctors, interpreting the questions and answers between them and my mother, but not understanding the diagnosis when it came. As it turned out, she was ill from malnutrition, and the tuberculosis in her eyes returned.

Mom had to go on disability leave before the age of forty. Doctors forbid her to work, but disability pay was very low, so she disobeyed the orders and worked on the side to supplement her income. Her side job was to do laundry - by hand - for a well-to-do family friend. It turned out the friend was her friend from school, Valentina, whose husband had a lucrative side job as a dental technician, and even though side jobs were not permitted, they would often mean the difference between poverty and survival.

I spent most of my summer holidays with my mother in Valentina's apartment while she was working. Sometimes I would go to the nearby park to play, but I would return after a short while to try and help her clean up before we went home. I vividly remember a day when my mother was doing the laundry and her knuckles were bleeding from washing a mountain of clothes by hand.

Sometimes I would get very hungry and would ask my mother for food. There was food in the fridge, but Mom - being so proud and honest - did not get me food from Valentina's fridge. Instead, she told me to be patient; she said we would be going home soon and would have something to eat there.

To this day, I can still recall the acute pain of hunger. When I think of my past life, sad memories come back, but when I look around and see where I am today, I am thankful to God for the strength he gave me so that my children do not have to ever know or feel that pain of hunger.

After we moved into the new apartment, Aunt Petra got a job and moved out. One day when I was about nine or ten years old, we ran out of food and money. Mom sent me all the way across the city to Aunt Petra's house. The ride was long, but luckily I had to take only one street car. Aunt Petra gave me a few potatoes to take home. She did not have much, but if she did have some food, she would share it with us. She worked three shifts in a factory where they made balls for children, and by this time she was already married and had two children, a boy and a girl. Often, I think back to this time and cannot believe that I travelled one hour one way, and then back, just for a few potatoes. At the time it made sense. We were hungry, and we did what we could to relieve our hunger.

Something that seems funny now, but awful at the time, happened one day when Mom and I were visiting Aunt Petra at her house. I needed to go to the bathroom, so I went to the outhouse in the backyard while my mother waited for me at the door. The toilet was old and made out of rotten wood. When I got my feet on the wooden seat, it broke, and I fell down the hole. I screamed, but of-course my mother couldn't hear me, so I continued screaming for about ten more minutes, which seemed like hours. I was desperately holding on to the wooden edges of the toilet, terrified that the whole thing would break and I would fall all the way down the hole and die, covered in excrement. What a terrible way to die!

Finally, the next-door neighbour heard my screams, and motioned from over the fence to my mother, to get me out from the outhouse. After this terrible incident, I had to bathe over and over again until I felt clean, and after that, I fell, exhausted, into a deep sleep until the next morning.

When I was in my early teens, I made a new friend. Her name was Sultana. She lived in our neighbourhood with her parents and four siblings. Sultana and her family turned out to be the most honest and compassionate people I had ever met. This brings me to another unforgettable story, which I still think about often.

Sultana's family of seven were as poor as we were. Her mother worked for the bread factory and her father was a concrete worker. For most of us food was scarce. A big family had its advantages, because there were more people available to wait in line outside stores, or to wait for food trucks to come. Whenever Sultana's family was able to buy meat, she would run over to our place and try to convince me to come over to their apartment, yelling from the top of her lungs: "Come! We have meat!"

Her family would wait for me to arrive before they started to eat. Everyone was so excited that there was no time to stop and think of a recipe to cook the meat. Sultana's mother would cut up the meat in stew like pieces, and fry them in a big pan. Once the meat was fried, she would place the pan in the middle of the table and we would all eat together. I can still remember the delicious taste of this meat. I think it tasted so good because we did not eat meat often. There are no words to express my feelings when I think about this story. Looking back, I realize how amazing and generous these people were. In spite of the fact that this was a big family, they didn't hesitate to share the little they had with another person. I was lucky enough to be that other person.

Not everyone was like them. These people were unique and very special. I cherish the time I spent with my friend Sultana and her family, and I will never forget them.

Later, when we became teenagers, Sultana and I became like twin sisters. We were always together. If one of us were asked to go on a date, we would first call the other and ask to go together on the date. The guys at that time did not mind if the girl brought her friend long.

One time, I was ill with a fever; it was so bad I thought I might die, so I told Sultana that she could have my clothes and whatever little things I owned. She thanked me but said not to worry, because I wouldn't die just from a fever. Sometimes, we would forget for a little while about the hard life that we had.

Because poverty dominated the whole country, most people were not as generous as my friends. Lack of food and freedom, and financial hardship, shapes people differently. Some become extraordinary and some the opposite. One day my mother sent me to buy bread. I was standing in line at the grocery store and a girl from the neighbourhood (we knew almost everyone from our neighbourhood because we did not drive; we walked everywhere and bumped into the same people who lived in the same area all their lives) walked up to me and struck up a conversation. I was always very polite and timid as a child. Some of the aggressive children saw this as weakness and took advantage. After a few minutes, the neighbourhood girl ripped my necklace (which had been my great-grandmother's and held much sentimental value) from my neck and ran off. Later, my mother took me to the girl's house and tried to get the necklace back, but we were unsuccessful.

When I was eight years old, one of my mother's deaf friends gave birth to a baby girl. She lived in the same area so she asked me to move in to help her. At first, when the baby cried, I would wake her mother up so she could feed her. After a while, I didn't bother waking her up. I would get up, heat the milk and change the baby. In the morning, I had to get up to go to school. It seemed natural to me - to help someone who needed help. It never crossed my mind that as a child I should go out and play, as any other child would.

And then after school, I would help in the kitchen. I will always remember the words the deaf lady's father said to me, while I was cleaning green beans: "Whoever wants to eat has to work; work for food."

CHAPTER FOUR

LIFE IN ROMANIA

A short while after we moved into the apartment, my mother met a man through her friends. He was from a village over 100 kilometers north-east of Bucharest. There was a law in Romania which prevented people from the countryside moving into the cities. The only way around it was if they married a city person. The police kept tabs on people by checking their ID, which was an identification booklet and had the person's photo, date and place of birth and address on it. It looked like a mini passport. The police authorities had the right to check this ID anywhere and anytime, and they did it often. If someone from the countryside was found in a city, they were arrested and investigated.

After a long time, the man convinced my mother to marry him. For him, it was a marriage of convenience, but for my mother it turned out to be a marriage of disappointment. After they married, he was allowed to move into the city and he moved into our apartment. He got a job at the railway factory as a locksmith. After he was paid, he would spend the money eating out alone and he would never contribute to the household. Mom and I remained as hungry as we had always been. Mom also suspected that he was cheating on her.

He adopted me, though I never found out why my mother agreed to this. I was given his last name, and because I was so young, I never knew what my last name was at birth.

One night when I was twelve years old, while I was sleeping, he tried to take my pyjamas off and molest me. My mother woke up and screamed, and I woke up in a bed of tears. Mother went to the police station to report him, but she was told that this was a domestic problem and they could not interfere. We stayed with a friend for a while but after a few weeks we had no choice but to return home.

I had recurring nightmares after that; these nightmares only stopped a few years ago. My terrifying dreams were always the same; it felt like I was actually raped. I would wake up in a sweat, crying. After sitting up for a few minutes, I said to myself, "Oh my God, he actually raped me!" Once I was fully awake, my mind would clear and then I would say: "Thank you God, for not letting him rape me."

Later, my mother told me that right after she married this man, Grandmother warned her that he was trying to touch me inappropriately. I was too young to remember this. My mother regretted that she did not believe my grandmother. She repeatedly said how guilty she felt, as she thought she could have saved me from going through this terrible incident.

After this time in my life, I started to suffer a sense of dread and fear. I didn't know at the time that what I was experiencing was anxiety, but this was a condition that was to continue throughout my life.

On summer vacations, my mother sent me to my grandmother's house in the country. This is where I was the happiest, as I could play with children my age or close to my age. My grandmother was very generous and kind to whomever she met. She was unique; one of a kind. We would play outside and at lunch or dinnertime Grandmother would call all of us kids (not just myself) into her house to eat. She didn't always have food, but whenever she did have it, she was generous, although when she didn't, no one offered to help her. I am forever thankful to my grandmother for the fond memories she created for me.

I used to call my grandmother "Mama" because she could hear me and I wanted so much to be able to be heard when

I said "Mama." She never went to school, but she was intelligent and I would call her a "true lady." She was very respectful and mindful of all the people she met. We had a very special relationship.

One sunny spring morning when I was four years old, Grandmother took me to the daycare at my mom's factory. We rode the streetcar to get there, and as we were getting closer to the daycare, I started to get anxious. I would have preferred to stay with her for the day. We arrived at the bus stop across from the daycare, where there was a stall with watermelons for sale. Grandmother knew how much I enjoyed watermelons, so to make me feel better, she bought one and smashed it open. We found a place to sit by a fence and we ate the watermelon together. It felt so good to be eating next to her, and it felt as I was floating on air and as if we were alone, just me and her. People around us became invisible. When she took me back to the daycare, I didn't feel so sad anymore.

Just before I started grade five, my mother found out about a boarding school for me. I qualified to attend because mother's income was very low and also because of her infirmity. Other children, like "C", who became my best friend in school, got in because her mother died. Her father had to work and could not provide proper care for her. The school was an impressive building; in-fact it was a castle. *Bogdan* Petriceicu Hasdeu, a writer, historian and politician, built the castle in memory of his daughter, writer Iulia Hasdeu, who died when she was just 18 years old. In 1929 the castle was converted into a school.

I went to classes and lived in the boarding school from Monday to Saturday. Sunday was the only day we could go home, if we behaved. The dormitories were large, with fifteen to twenty wire-framed beds. Sometimes the base of the bed, on which the thin mattress lay, would fall down during the night, and in the morning we would laugh when we saw one of the girls still sleeping on the ground in the sunken bed. Our caregivers were called *pedagogues*, and they were very strict. After the lights went out, the tough girls would verbally abuse the weaker girls. I was one of those weaker girls.

In spite of the fact that I was bullied, I was happy that at least food was provided and I was not hungry anymore. Every morning at seven o' clock we were woken by a loud whistle coming from the pedagogue, and we had to get up and stand straight by the side of our beds. We would exercise at the pedagogue's loud command; she would count down from fifteen minutes, and by the end of the fifteen minutes we would be panting and sweating.

We were timed while washing and dressing. Whomever did not make it in time was punished by the caregivers. I did not realize at the time that this was abuse. Once, at dinner, one of the students couldn't finish her soup. The caregiver picked up the bowl and poured the soup over her head.

In class the abuse continued. Students talking during class would get straps from teachers. I only got the straps once. I was so terrified and hurt by the experience that I obeyed them fully after that. This was the first time I had ever had to live with strangers, and fear ruled; fear of being bullied at every level; fear of being humiliated or punished; fear of being the weakest, and fear of everyone and everything. I missed my mother a lot, but most of all I was worried about her, asking myself "how is she going to manage without me?" My mother had a hard time as well, as she could not see me all week, but she knew that at least I was getting three meals a day.

"C" and I became best friends and later became rebellious together. There was a guard at the front door, so we could not go outside the school unless we had a note from the caregivers. "C" and I tried to sneak out to meet friends and sometimes we got caught. As punishment we were not allowed to go home on Sundays. Mother would come to school to pick me up but had to go back home without me.

One time we snuck out, and on our return thought we had got away with it, but we had a hard time getting back into the school. We called out to our friends who were up in the dormitories, and they threw us bed sheets to help us climb up and get in through the windows. Half way through, we fell back on the ground and the caregivers heard us. We were caught and separated, but somehow we found a way to be together again.

I was twelve years old when one of our teachers asked me if I wanted an English pen pal. Gladly I agreed and she gave me the address of an English lady. This is when my friendship with Ada began. Ada was in her thirties at the time, with three daughters who were around my age. We corresponded for many years and today we are still friends. I was not able to meet her at the time because of Romanian laws, which did not allow Romanian citizens to visit other countries. Every two years, people were allowed to apply for a passport, but it was not guaranteed they would get one. Not too many people were approved to get a passport. I knew that I had no chance of getting one, so I didn't even try.

To me, Romania felt like a big, oppressive jail. I was suffocating, and often anxiety would engulf me. We had English classes in school, but we only learned the basics. Ada would correct and send my letters back to me, so my English language could get better. I wrote to her about my mother and my life at school, but I was careful not to write about the communist system that existed in my country. Every letter that came from another country was opened and read by authorities. If they found criticism, the police were sent to the house and the person brought in for interrogation. Most of the time this resulted in punishment, such as jail or beatings.

I used to ask Ada to describe her house and what kind of things she did with her family. I felt as if her letters transported me to a different world. The English language I learned, even though basic, was useful when I later went to live in Canada.

I will always be grateful to Ada for being there for me during my school years, through her letters. She offered me encouragement and hope. Thanks to her I started to dream that one day I could escape from Romania. I kept asking myself: what grown-up with a family of her own would take the time to write and console a poor, young Romanian girl? She had the heart and patience to listen to my stories, and I am so thankful and happy she did. Today, she is the only person left who knows my life step by step, as she was there in spirit. We corresponded for thirty years without meeting in person.

When I finally met her, I was married with children, living in Canada. I travelled to England to meet her. She lived about two hours away from London by train, in a charming town. Ada and her husband came to meet me at the train station. I instantly recognized her and of-course felt like I had known her forever. As soon as I saw her house, I was stunned to see that it looked the same as I imagined it when I was a child.

Ada and I at Niagara Falls, during one of her visits.

The day after I arrived, a newspaper reporter called to ask questions so he could publish an article about us, as he heard about us being pen pals for many years and that we had just met in person for the first time. We arranged a meeting and he interviewed us. I have the newspaper article to this day.

I had an amazing time meeting and visiting with my English friend and her husband. They took me to visit castles and art galleries. After I returned to Canada, we continued our friendship. A few years after my visit, her husband passed away, and after that Ada came to visit me in Canada a few times. One of her visits was when she came to my daughter Jennifer's wedding. We are still good friends today. Every time she writes to me, she signs off "Love, Mama," so I feel that we are actually family.

I often made friends on my travels. At the end of that first trip to visit Ada and her family, I stayed in London for a few days before catching my flight home. Whilst waiting for the "stop and go" tourist bus, I met a friendly woman called Susan who was from South Africa. We ended up taking the bus tour together, and have stayed in touch ever since. We are still friends and Susan has visited me in Canada.

Susan and I at the CN Tower in Toronto

CHAPTER FIVE

ENDINGS AND BEGINNINGS

Through the Mute and Deaf Club, Mother met new deaf friends who were visiting from Poland. One of the remarkable things about deaf people is that they make friends no matter where they are in the world. One of the Polish family became so close to us that every time they came to Romania they stayed at our place.

Poland was also a communist a country, but it was less strict and the people there were more free and could travel more easily. Unlike Romanians, Polish people were allowed to travel to other communist countries easily. Romanians were allowed to apply for a single-use passport every two years, but were not guaranteed they would be granted one.

At the suggestion of our Polish friends, we applied to go and visit them. After being declined three times, we finally received our passports. I was seventeen years old. We were excited and curious to see what another country would be like.

Our friends were very hospitable and we had a great time. While in Poland I made friends with both girls and boys. We promised each other that we would write and visit each other. One of the boys kept his promise, and shortly afterwards he came to visit me in Romania.

Through my mom's deaf and mute friends I met a "hearing" family in Poland. Their daughter Bozena became my best friend. Being the same age, we had much in common. I didn't understand the Polish language at the time so we tried to communicate by saying words in different languages or by using sign language, at which I was an expert.

Bozena took me along to a few family parties. One time, she and her parents took me to a family communion celebration. Even the priest was invited and sat at the table with us. Bozena showed me off, telling everyone that in just a couple of weeks I had already learned many Polish words.

One day she asked me to go to a party at her cousin's house. I didn't understand at the time what kind of party. In Poland, just as in Romania, most people did not live in big houses; they lived in apartments. This family lived in a house, although it was only a two-room house. It turned out that the party was held for a father and son's "Name Day" (in Poland, Name Day was more popular and more celebrated than birthdays).

Dinner was served in the two different rooms on two big tables which had been placed in each room. One room was for adults (relatives and friends) to enjoy delicious homemade food, and to talk; and the other room for the younger people. We had a great time.

One of the boys, Roman, lived in that house and is the boy who eventually became my husband (though of-course I didn't even think of marriage at the time). At the beginning I did not like him much as he was drinking too much alcohol; and he asked me to go out with him while his girlfriend was sitting right next to him at the same table as us.

I was the only one at the party who was not drinking, which was not easy because Polish people seemed to take offence if a person refused a drink in their home. They would accuse you of thinking you were better than they were.

At the time, a lot of Polish people, especially men, would drink excessively. On payday, men would often go straight to the liquor store to buy a bottle or two of vodka. They would drink until they passed out and would end up sleeping on the street or on a bench in the park. Many times they would get robbed, and the next morning they would they would return home to their family with empty pockets. Wives would have to work so that they could support their children, and sometimes their older parents. I witnessed this lifestyle for myself later, whilst living in Poland for a few months before emigrating.

After three weeks of having fun, meeting people my age and making good friends, I went back home, giddy with good memories. Once I arrived home, to my surprise Roman wrote me a letter telling me he wanted to visit me in Romania the following month.

When I met Roman he already had a drinking problem. I did not realize then that it would be a lifetime struggle and hardship for both of us. I was young and inexperienced, believing that his problem would eventually go away. I believe that he loved me, but in a strange way, as he was very jealous and controlling - especially after getting drunk. Often after each argument he would apologize and convince me that things would be different and that this type of behaviour would not be repeated. I think that at the time he believed it.

In Romania, while under Ceausescu's dictatorship, there were so many restrictions. For example, people were not allowed to interact with foreigners. If we happened to talk to a foreign tourist we were supposed to go to the police station and report how we had met and what we discussed with that person.

We were not allowed to have in our possession any foreign money. Ordinary people were becoming informants for the police in exchange for being allowed to break the law. This made it very hard for me to date my future husband.

Romania was (and still is, I believe) a severely corrupted country; only people with money could bribe the police and government so they could get away with breaking the law. Few people had money. Mostly, it was members of the communist party who had money and they would get away with terrible things, including rape and abuse. They were also able to buy foreign items and sell them on the black market in order to make more money. They had their own shops where they could buy anything they wanted, including food. These shops were not available to the public.

Because of poverty and the harshness of life, ordinary people were also mean to us, especially to me. Some boys in the neighbourhood called me names, and because I was dating a foreigner I was also called a "whore." After our engagement, the people in most neighbourhoods said that Roman was taking advantage of me and would never marry me.

When Roman was visiting us, my mom let him stay at in our apartment. Some neighbours - being informants - would report us and he had to pay heavy fines. The worst thing was the fact that the police started to harass me and ordered me to be present at the police station every morning, and threatened me with jail.

According to the law at the time we were allowed to date a foreigner only if we were engaged to him or her. "Engaged" meant to register (by making an application to the government asking permission to get married to that person). The waiting period was between one and two years. Not all of the applications were approved. In fact, I met girls who already had children with their foreign fiancés and were still not approved to get married, and therefore could not leave the country.

While waiting for my engagement approval, the police kept ordering me to go to the police station to be interrogated; this would last for eight to nine hours a day. It was very tiring and stressful, but I had to be strong. They were trying to convince me to change my mind. They would say things like, "why would you want to marry and go away with him? Do you know that he will use you as a prostitute?" I knew it was not true and I kept repeating to them that I didn't care.

The secret police would follow us everywhere. One night we went to a restaurant. As we left and got into a taxi, the secret police stopped the car and ordered us to get out. They asked why I was with Roman. I explained that we were engaged; they asked for our papers to prove it. We did not have the papers with us, so Roman went to the apartment to retrieve them while I was taken to the police station.

At the police station, I saw five or six other women sitting at different desks, writing statements explaining why they too had been found with a foreigner. I assumed these women were prostitutes. One of them asked me who I was with and I replied, "My fiancé." One of them sneered and said, "Sure, we were with our fiancés as well!"

When Roman arrived with our papers, the women giggled and flirted with him. He thought they were office workers and greeted them appropriately. I had to explain to him why they were there. This memory still brings a smile to my face.

Around this time, Mom became very ill and was hospitalized. Doctors never told me that she was about to die, so until she actually died I was hoping she would come back home and live forever. Shortly before she passed away the hospital sent her home. They discharged her but no-one bothered to notify me that I could pick her up. She could barely walk as she took a bus and a street car to come home. She was alone.

I was walking down the street, and suddenly saw my mom walking very slowly towards me. At first I thought I was dreaming or imagining what I was seeing. As I watched her shuffling along the street, I said to myself, "no, this is impossible, she is in the hospital, and they can't let an ill person go out in the street like that." I helped her home and for three days and nights I took care of her without a wink of sleep. I would just doze off for five minutes at a time.

When our neighbour came to visit, my mom told her that she was dying but not to tell me. One night Mom got very ill, vomiting something that looked liked liver chopped up. I don't exactly know what it was, but that was what it looked like. I got scared and I didn't know what to do or how to help her. It was midnight. I went out and called an ambulance (we had no phone or car). We waited all night. The ambulance came in the morning and took her to the hospital. I went with her in the ambulance and when we arrived there, she was placed into a small room by herself. I didn't know it at the time, although it did feel strange to me, that when they place someone in a room by themselves it means that the person is just about to pass away. In normal circumstances, when someone was a patient in the hospital they would stay in a room with multiple beds, with other patients. There was no such thing as a "private room."

What happened next haunts me to this day, as it makes me feel guilty. A nurse came into the room and told me that I looked tired and should go home to get some rest and to come back in the afternoon. She told me she would give Mom something to ease her pain. While she was getting the needle ready, my mom was motioning something to me, but because she was weak I couldn't understand what she was trying to tell me. At the same time the cleaning lady came in and was trying to motion to me not to go home. I couldn't understand why one person was telling me to go and another was telling me to stay. I was confused and tired and didn't know what was going on. The nurse started to push me out of the door, and so I left. I started going down the stairs and heard my mom screaming. To this day I don't know if it was my imagination because I was tired or it was for real. I started to run down the stairs to get away from the screaming, which I thought I was imagining.

I went home to get some sleep and woke up to loud banging on the door. My mom's uncle was at the door telling me that my mom had just died. I told him that she was not dead because I had just left her at the hospital that morning. I was in shock; I kept saying, "I know she is sick but she will get better soon."

I had no idea. No one told me she was dying. Doctors were very secretive. On the way to the hospital that day I told myself and my mother's uncle that I didn't believe she was dead until I saw it with my own eyes. Before she died, while she was sick, my mom asked my fiancé to promise he would take care of me. She was afraid I would be left all alone. I was scared, but most of all heartbroken.

Ever since then, many times in my mind I have repeated the scene of what happened that night and I feel guilty. I understand now that she was trying to tell me to stay with her. I think she was scared to die all alone. I should have stayed, and I am mad at myself that I did not realize what she was saying and that I should have listened to the cleaning lady.

As I have got older, after speaking to many people who have lost close family members, I know that most people feel guilty for different reasons, blaming themselves for what they should have done but didn't do. I try to make myself feel better by thinking that this kind of thing is common. Deep down inside I still feel the pang and the pain of guilt.

I had no money to bury my mother, but my fiancé helped me and somehow we managed.

CHAPTER SIX

THE REFUGEE CAMP

consider myself lucky because after waiting for one year, I was approved by the government to get married. In my initial application I had to answer a question in which I was asked where I would be living after I got married. I said "maybe we will live in Romania." Why would they deny me that? I thought naively. They still declined. We got married at the City Hall in Bucharest and right after that I applied for a visitor's passport to Poland. I was declined again. I made an appointment with the government office. I told them, "I don't understand. I am his wife and I want to visit his family, who are now my family."

The only way to leave the country was to apply for permanent residence to Poland based on the fact that I was married to a Polish citizen. I had to wait another year to leave the country. I was given a special passport which was called a "passport for Romanian citizens living abroad." This gave me freedom.

At the same time friends of my mother's who were also deaf and mute had to go through the same thing. Genia, who was Polish, was married to my mom's Romanian friend. They got married under the same circumstances. They had a baby boy while living in Romania and by the time they left the country their son Robert was already seven years old.

I lived in Poland for three months. While living in Poland, I learned that we could go to live in one of the western countries where I could be free and have a better life for us and our future children.

We needed money; I soon learned that now I was free, I could take advantage of this by travelling to other countries where I could buy goods to sell in another country. Romania had a shortage of everything: food, clothes and everything else you can think of.

The first western country I ever visited was Austria. When I alighted from the train in Vienna and started to walk through the colourful city streets, I was mesmerized by its beauty. I had never seen anything like it. The city even smelled delicious, and as I inhaled its sweet aroma, I was amazed that such a place existed. I am not sure now if this was my imagination or if it was true. Maybe I was so enamoured with the colour, the beauty and the freedom, that I have romanticised the memory.

I walked on Maria Hilfer Strasse from the train station all the way to the city centre; it was a long way but time had ceased to exist for me. I was in a state of awe and wonder. By the time I got to the downtown area, it was dark outside. I bought myself a sausage or a hotdog (I don't remember exactly), and kept walking, until I realized I had to find a hotel room for the night. I spent the whole of the next day, still amazed, walking around Vienna.

For the short time I lived in Poland I would travel to Austria and Italy and go back to Romania to sell things that families were desperate for. People would give me a list of items they wanted or needed and I would make sure they got it. I didn't realize it at the time but I was becoming a kind of entrepreneur.

The visit to Austria was my first foray into entrepreneurship. I went there to buy products that I could later sell. Unfortunately, I lost all the money I had saved for my new business venture, buying items that were too expensive to make a profit when I sold them.

Later, some like-minded friends showed me where the Jewish market was, and it was there that I learned how to buy the same items for less, so that I was finally able to make a profit.

Our friends Genia and Nelu were doing the same thing. They were travelling back and forth to Romania from other countries so they could make some money to help pay for their escape to one of the western countries. They were taking their four-year-old son Robert along with them, and I remember being amazed at how smart he was. He was already speaking Romanian, Polish and sign language. He understood what was going on. Every time they crossed the border, the train would stop for the customs officers to get on, and Robert would be as nervous as his parents, his heart beating fast as the customs officers scanned the train and its passengers.

In sign language he would tell his parents, "We have to be careful so they don't find the stuff and the dollars." When his mom told me the story, it melted my heart and I felt so sad for the little boy. He reminded me of myself. He had to grow up fast and understand the cruel life that our communist country imposed on us. I so related to him. In the end they settled in Germany, where they live to this day.

As for us, we decided to go to a refugee camp in Austria. We had to follow the correct procedure: first we had to go to the police station in Vienna and surrender. The police took us in a minivan to the refugee camp which was located just outside Vienna in a small town called Traiskirchen.

The camp was composed of two buildings, five or six stories high, and one low building, which was the office. There was a high fence around the buildings and a gatehouse at the entrance. The buildings had run-down toilets and showers down the hallway, which were used by everyone.

We were interrogated at the camp for a long time. Finally, in the evening we were allowed to have something to eat. I was seven months pregnant and it was very tiring. The anxiety I had started to suffer years earlier showed itself again and I would often find myself silently battling a sense of dark apprehension and worry.

Men were separated from women and sent to the top floor. It was called quarantining. They were kept locked up for about three weeks. In that time they were checked out to see if they had a bad record. If they passed the check they were released to be with their wives. Men who had children or pregnant wives were allowed to stay together while the investigation was going on. We were lucky as we didn't have to be separated. I think that people with families were trusted more than single people.

Unsurprisingly, the food was unbearable. After all it was a refugee camp - and it felt like we were in jail. I couldn't help but cry when the inedible and disgusting-looking, colourless slop was placed in front of us. The only time that the food was acceptable was on a Thursday, when we were given a sandwich and a chocolate bar. Thursday was my favourite day.

Every morning the refugees would gather outside the camp at the street corner, where Austrian businessmen would drive up and pick some of them for work. My husband tried to get a job, but he was rarely chosen as he couldn't commit to work for a long period of time as I was expecting a baby and wanted to move to another town where we could live in a safer place.

I went to the camp office and explained my situation. They told me to be patient. There was a place about two hours away, close to Salzburg, where they would send families with children. We were promised a spot there as soon as one became available.

We were lucky as they sent us there before the baby was born. I couldn't believe it! We had a room all to ourselves so I could take care of the baby in private. The landscape was breathtaking, with mountains all around us. The baby would sleep in the carriage outside in fresh air even though it was winter time. European winters are milder than North American winters so we could enjoy taking the baby for walks in the beautiful mountains.

One time we came across a fast-running river which ran through the valley between the mountains, and we tried to fish. At one point, a man with a gun showed up yelling at us in German. This is when we realized we were trespassing on private land. We were shocked and scared, so we ran quickly back to the camp.

An emotional thing happened after I gave birth to our daughter. My Aunt Petra sent me a parcel from Romania. The parcel contained baby clothes and oranges. This made me cry.

In Romania, where stores were mostly empty, people still had to stand in line on the street in front of the store for days waiting for the trucks to arrive with food, clothes or anything at all. To keep warm they brought blankets with them; and family members would take it in turns to stay in line. My Aunt Petra had to stay in line on the street for two days to buy the oranges she sent me.

In Austria, the stores were full with food and everything you wished for. There was no need for her to send me oranges, but Aunt Petra was not aware of this. She thought all other countries were in the same situation as Romania. The irony of this, and my aunt's sacrifice, made me sad.

Much later, in around 1987, Aunt Petra came to visit us in Canada, and the first thing she asked me was if we could buy potatoes in Canada. I realized how much worse the situation had become in Romania since I left. I was shocked. When I had lived in Romania, at least I could buy potatoes, if nothing else.

The very next day I took her to the grocery store. In the meat department, tears started rolling down her face. She couldn't believe how much meat was available for us to buy right away. She was amazed by everything she saw in Canada.

This goes to show how people were kept in the dark. In Romania we did not get any news from outside our country. The news and newspapers were only relating stories about the communist party. Some people were listening illegally on the radio to Free Europe. This channel was reporting news from all over Europe. If anyone was caught listening to this channel they would be arrested and punished. People had no freedom of speech, no freedom to listen to worldwide news, no freedom to travel; no freedom at all.

Among many other things that were illegal in Romania was abortion. You probably think this was because of religion, but no. Communist people did not believe in religion, God or church. The head of the country wanted population growth. Our dictator (the country's president) made the following law: every family had to have at least four children. After four children, women were allowed to have an abortion. Because of poverty, most people in Romania had only one child, some had two at most. Young families couldn't afford to have kids as there were no means to feed or clothe them, so there were many illegal abortions going on.

Abortions were performed by women who were not qualified nurses and did not have any medical training or experience at all. They were provoking the abortion with coat hangers which were not sterilized. Women would get infections and die. When they were taken to the hospital these women were interrogated as to whom had performed the abortion. Even though they were about to die, help was not given until they confessed. Most women would not confess and would therefore die. I personally knew a few women that this happened to. My best friend's older sister died after she had an illegal abortion. She could have been saved, but nurses refused to help her as she would not inform them of the woman who had performed the abortion.

CHAPTER SEVEN

THE ROAD TO CANADA

I know is hard to believe that we have some good memories from a refugee camp, but we did. Despite the hardships we faced, and the bouts of anxiety I endured, it was not all bad. We made good friends, connecting through our common experiences; we came from similar countries and we could understand each other. We all shared stories from our own countries, and we would spend time together, going for mountain walks in the daytime, and playing cards in the evenings.

Once we moved to the new camp, my husband tried to get a job but there were two reasons why he couldn't: we were in a small town where jobs were scarce, and also because at the time western European people were prejudiced against immigrants.

Unfortunately, my husband had a bad temper and was abusive. At the time, I thought it was normal for marriages to have their ups and down, and I didn't question it. Roman never got a job in Austria, so we had to accept living on what little the camp had to offer.

In the camp, we made friends with a Romanian couple who were waiting to immigrate to the U.S. We would play cards together after dinner. They had a three-year-old daughter so I was relieved to get advice on how to care for my baby once she arrived. I was starting to get anxious and nervous as my due date had passed.

Finally one morning after breakfast my water broke and because I was so young and inexperienced, I was confused. I ran to our friend's room and banged on the door until I woke her up. I told her "I don't know what's happening!" I was scared to see water coming out. She smiled and told me not to worry because this meant I was going to have the baby.

My husband went to the office to call the ambulance and we were taken to the next town where the hospital was located. When the doctor came to check on me, I heard a woman screaming in the next room, which terrified me. After a couple of minutes I heard the baby crying from the same room. I then understood why she had been screaming. My mother had never talked to me about such things. Parents did not think it was proper to talk about pregnancy and labour. During the pregnancy, I was never seen by a doctor.

At the hospital, I was told that I might need a Caesarean section. The doctor brought in a machine (now I know it was an ultrasound machine) and after checking he confirmed that a Caesarean operation was necessary to give birth. It's hard to describe how I felt when I saw my baby. I couldn't believe she was mine, and how beautiful she was with her dark eyes, dark hair, white skin and rosy cheeks. She looked like a mini-Snow White. Of-course I kept counting her little fingers and toes and I was relieved to see she had ten of each.

After the baby was born, I shared a room with three other new moms. They were Austrian and I couldn't understand a word of what they were saying. I had to stay in the hospital for three weeks (required at the time after a Caesarean section), and I quickly learned a few German words. Babies were kept in a separate room and were brought in to the mom's room only for feeding. Because of the Caesarean section I was not given food for a week (doctors didn't think was good to eat after an operation); only liquids. I was very hungry and when food was brought in for the other ladies the smell made me even hungrier. One day when the baby was with me a doctor came in to check on us. She stopped by my bed and admired my baby, saying "what a beautiful baby." According to her, she had never seen a dark-haired baby in person, as most Austrian babies had either blonde or red hair.

Family members and husbands would visit their loved ones and their babies. This made me feel lonely and I fell into a depression. My husband couldn't come to visit us as he couldn't afford the bus fare from the camp to the hospital. Because the baby was brought to me only at feeding time, I was missing both my husband and my baby. I was alone and very sad, crying mostly at night, when everyone was sleeping. The three weeks I stayed there felt much longer.

Once back in the camp and with our friends, we all gathered and celebrated the birth of our baby. Austria is a very picturesque country with snow-capped mountains, pretty landscapes, clean air and mild winters. In spite of the snow the weather was superb and the sun was shining every day. We believed in the benefits of fresh air, so every day we would go for a walk with the baby in the stroller through the mountains.

A young Austrian lady, Ingrid, came into the camp to teach us English language. After I gave birth to my daughter, she came to our room to see her. She was fascinated with our baby, but I could see the sadness in her eyes when she walked into our room and saw how little we had. She felt really sorry for us, because we had a baby and not much to provide for her. We didn't feel that way, because we didn't know any other way, and we were happy to have a healthy and beautiful baby girl. Ingrid went with my husband to an employment office and asked if they had a job for him.

She was asked by the employment officer why was she getting involved with people like us. She turned around and left the office without speaking. Once we were together back in the camp, she told us how sad and ashamed she was that her own people were so prejudiced.

Though it was not ideal, I have cherished memories from that time. Recently, for the first time since I left, I went back to Austria for a visit. It was very emotional and beautiful. It was incredible to be there feeling free and not to worry about where I would be going next.

While in the refugee camp, we applied to go to the U.S. or Canada and we agreed that the country that approved us first would be the one we went to. Canada was the first to accept us, and after an interview at the Canadian embassy in Vienna, we immigrated to Canada. At the embassy we were told we would be living in Winnipeg, a city with very cold winters. The embassy's representative asked us if we were OK with that. We happily said, "Yes!" We didn't care what kind of weather we were going to live in, as long as it was Canada. (We were also reluctant to ask for another city, such as Toronto or Vancouver, as we thought we might be denied immigration altogether).

It was a very joyous day when we received the letter from the Canadian embassy, saying we could go and live in Canada. According to the hospital doctor, the baby had to be at least three months old to travel on an aeroplane. We got sponsored by a religious non-profit organization called Caritas, which paid for our plane tickets with a verbal promise from us that we would pay the money back whenever we got a job in Canada, so they could help other immigrants coming after us. We were thankful for the help and of-course, we paid it back as soon as we could.

When the time came to leave, we said goodbye to our friends and boarded the plane to our new life. The weather conditions were bad so we had to take a detour and stop in New York. On the airplane I met a smiling American lady who was very friendly. She told me her husband was a football player and she was going back home to New York. I was not familiar with American football at the time and I thought she was referring to soccer. As most of you know, in Europe "football" means "soccer".

We arrived in the free land of Canada, with a baby and one suitcase. Finally! Oh, what a relief! We were determined to work hard and make the "Canadian" dream come true.

We had to start our life all over again. Life was hard but we didn't give up hope. We didn't know anybody, and there were no jobs for people with no work experience in Canada. For our first three weeks in the country we stayed in a rundown hotel, sponsored by the Canadian government.

It was February, one of the coldest months of the winter, especially in Winnipeg. In the freezing, windy weather, with a map in his hand, my husband had to walk the streets of Winnipeg looking for a place to live and work. I could speak very basic English but my husband did not speak English at all.

Leaving the pristine beauty of Austria and finding myself in the middle of a harsh Winnipeg winter – a grey, grim city – was a shock that I hadn't expected.

Despite being glad to be in our new country, I felt overwhelmed and fearful. There were so many obstacles to face: the freezing weather, learning a new language, finding a job, and the worry of raising our family in this new country where we knew no-one. I started to suffer with crippling migraines, sometimes to the point where I was unable to drive or function normally. If I was driving and a migraine came on, I would have to stop the car.

I did not know this was a form of anxiety. I just felt strange; different. My heart would beat so fast that I felt sure I was having a heart attack. I did not know what was happening to me, until much later when I learned about panic attacks.

I have since then come to understand more about anxiety, and through understanding and meditation, I have learned to cope with it, although I don't believe it can ever be fully cured. I know this because I still occasionally awake in the middle of the night with a racing heart and an uncontrollable sense of panic.

With the help of the government office, we found a place to live on the main floor of an old house. My husband found a job as a millwright worker and we also managed to get an evening job cleaning offices together in a building downtown. We would take our beautiful baby daughter Athena, and place her in a baby chair on top of a desk while we worked.

During the years we lived in Winnipeg, I worked in an egg factory, a restaurant, a bank and a real estate office as a salesperson.

While working in real estate I paired up with another lady (Ella) from the office and together we would walk around neighbourhoods, knocking on doors and asking if people wanted to sell their house. We worked well together and we reached the sales goals we were supposed to. Clients loved us because we were quite a pair. I was the funny one while my colleague was more serious. Word spread, and people started asking for the "two great real estate ladies." We did whatever worked to make a sale.

Our partnership ended when I moved to Toronto, where I no longer worked in real estate. Instead, I became an insurance broker. Last year after twenty-nine years living apart in two different cities, Ella got in touch with me and we have now renewed our friendship.

In Winnipeg, we bought a brand new house and there we met our next door neighbours who were a lovely family; the couple were around our age and they also had two children and were expecting another one. We became good friends and through them, I learned to speak English.

Looking back, I wonder how I managed so many things at once, but while the kids were growing up, I finished college and a few courses at the University of Manitoba while working part time. It was hard and sometimes felt impossible to continue, but I kept going. I realized that if in need, anyone can accomplish anything they want. All that is needed is determination and a strong work ethic.

After my tough upbringing; the poverty and hardship that I endured; living in a refugee camp; and moving halfway across the world, I could never have imagined or predicted that one day I would be running my own business, but that is exactly what I ended up doing.

In 1989 I was approached by an insurance company who suggested I open my own office. I went on to become a very successful salesperson, and because of this, I was rewarded with numerous overseas trips. I travelled extensively – to Spain, Hawaii, the Caribbean, many U.S. cities, and on lavish European cruises. I earned these unforgettable trips with hard work and perseverance, but they are trips I could never have dreamed of in my previous life, and I am truly grateful for the opportunities that came my way and made these experiences possible.

I believe in the saying "you can do and be anything you want." I feel I am proof of the philosophy behind these words.

CHAPTER EIGHT

MY LIFE

As time went on, my husband's drinking problem got worse and so did his verbal and physical abuse towards me.

We sold our house and decided to move from Winnipeg to Toronto, hoping that his habits would change and that our relationship would improve.

Mostly he would drink on the weekends, but when he drank, he drank to excess. His problem was genetic, I felt; from his Polish upbringing.

His temper, rage and jealousy became extreme; to the point where he was hitting me and ripping all my clothes off so I couldn't leave the house. The abuse became unbearable. One day he hit me in the head and the blow was so bad that I had to go to hospital. The police charged him, and issued a restraining order so that he couldn't come anywhere near my house. He was released from jail the very next day.

From that day on we separated. During our marriage my husband liked to spend money and buy expensive things, including cars, on credit. I was left with all the debt, but I didn't care as I was free of abuse.

At the time the mortgage interest in Canada was high and home sales went down. Our mortgage payment was high as well, so my husband decided to sign over the house to me, as he did not want to take over a big mortgage payment.

Once again I was very scared. I didn't know how I was going to pay my bills. I made an appointment with the bank manager and explained my situation. I asked for a chance to get on my feet. I asked for six months to try to get more jobs, so I could start making mortgage payments again. I promised that if I couldn't start paying in six months, I would sell the house, even if I was going to lose money.

The bank manager agreed and I went looking for more work. By that time I was already working in an insurance office. I found two more jobs cleaning offices, evenings and weekends. I did everything in my power to put food on the table and keep my kids warm.

My determination to survive and stay in my house with my children paid off. I was able to pay off my bills. Soon, I advanced in my insurance job, and because I was good in sales I made more money, and didn't need to clean offices anymore. I was able to buy a bigger house without selling my first one. I had worked hard to keep it, so I did not want to ever let it go.

Four years after my marriage ended my husband passed away in an accident.

It was soon after his passing that I opened my own insurance office. I finally had time to do the things I always wanted to, such as travelling, reading and looking at some real estate.

For the first nine years in Canada I still had no desire to go back to Romania as I was very bitter about the hard life we had there and the freedom that had been taken away from us.

Finally, though, the nostalgia kicked in. I began missing the places I grew up in, as well as my friends, Aunt Petra and my cousins.

I was nervous to go back but I still risked it. I had escaped the country, so I was considered a political refugee and the communists had a way of dealing with these kinds of people. While visiting, I distinctively remember people telling me to be careful as things could go wrong. I was told that communists can make people disappear. I was told that something could happen to me and they would make it look like an accident. After being told this, I was very nervous every time I crossed the street.

I will always remember the first time I went back home. From the airport I took a taxi to my aunt's apartment. On the way to her place, I kept seeing crowds of people gathered in different places. I asked the taxi driver if something bad happened; an accident perhaps? He told me that the crowds were people waiting in line for trucks to come with food. That is when it hit me and I remembered how it used to be. I had supposed that after being away for nine years things had changed for the better. Instead it had changed for the worse.

Aunt Petra and my cousins were excited to see me. Traditional Romanian food was cooked for me as they wanted me to feel like I was home again. My aunt took me into the kitchen and showed me a whole piece of salami and cheese which she said was for me only. I knew right away that they would have had to wait in line outside the stores to buy the food, so I refused and said "no, that's not only for me, it is for you to eat. I will go back to Canada and have plenty of it." Of-course she did not want to hear any of it.

My cousin Cristina told me how people would take chairs and blankets and stay all night outside stores, without knowing when the food would arrive, but still did it every day. Sometimes they would wait for two or three days until the food truck would come. The sad part was that if people were not in the first rows in line, they risked not getting any food at all. There was never enough food for everyone because of corruption. People with money would pay the store workers under the table and get more food that they should get.

For my cousin Cristina, waiting in line became a habit. She used to wait all night and would tell jokes to pass the time. Cristina is very funny. I always thought that she should be a comedian. On my first night, we stayed up until morning and talked about the past; about our times together. We also reminisced about our grandmother whom we both loved and grew up with. Each of us, at different times, had the same experiences with our grandmother. Cristina stayed behind with Grandma after I left the country, so we compared notes. Sometimes, our grandmother was funny as well. We were reminiscing about the way she was, and the things she used to do and say. We were amazed to find out that Grandma did the same things with both of us. We cried and laughed together telling each other how much we missed her. It was a memorable night.

I am a nostalgic and emotional person. All the years away from where I was born and raised, I had been thinking about my family and about the friends and neighbours I had left behind. I went to see my old school, which now is no longer a boarding school. Now it is a regular high school. The next day I started looking for my childhood friends and especially I wanted to see my best friend "C" from boarding school.

I was very nervous and excited to see my friend after fifteen years. I was happy to hear that she was well known and respected in the film industry as she worked as a movie producer and editor. She made little money but her job was considered prestigious. Prestige was very important in Romania. Once we got together it was like old times. We couldn't stop talking and reminiscing about the past and what went on in our lives after I left the country.

I also went to visit my old neighbour and friend, Mihaela. She had become a doctor. Her mother used to be the principal of our school. Mihaela and her parents were happy to see me. She told me her husband was a doctor as well and he had escaped to Germany. Mihaela and her son were waiting to be approved by the government to move and reunite with her husband. She told me how much she admired my courage to escape the country as soon as I finished high school. She wished she didn't stay behind and waste so many years suffering. I thank God for giving me strength to do that. I realised that I had come a long way.

The communist leader of the country was keeping people in the dark by not allowing them to find out how people in other countries lived. When I was growing up in Romania we only had two TV channels which only showed the president talking about himself and how great he was, as well as political songs praising him.

The president, in his speeches, kept emphasising that in the western countries, people were killed every day and everyone owned a gun and so these countries were very dangerous. There were a couple of exceptions on the TV. In the evenings, for half an hour, on one of the two channels, a cartoon show was allowed. Most of the time the shows were repeats. In schools, teachers were forced to tell children that our county had the best president and that we were living in the greatest country ever. As well, teachers had to tell children that there was no such thing as Santa Claus and God did not exist. Some teachers who refused to follow these rules were fired.

I met a couple in the refugee camp who were both teachers and had to leave the country as they were fired because they did not obey these rules. As a result of all the brainwashing, people's mentality was so much different than those living in western countries. I guess I changed, because when I went back I could see a big difference in thinking and behaviour between myself and people still living in Romania. The majority of the people were still thinking that those living in western countries were all rich and that they should bring them clothes and other material things. In other words they were under the impression that "money was falling from trees".

When my grandmother was still alive and I was living in Canada, I used to phone her every month. As soon as I had a job, I sent her money every month as she did not have a pension. People in the village found out and word got around. Every time she left the house they used to yell after her "how are you today American old lady?" People were invidious and a couple of times she got robbed.

One time when I was talking to her on the phone she told me something I had said when I was a little girl. I had said, "Don't worry Mama because once I grow up, I'll get a job and give you money. You will never be hungry again". I couldn't remember saying that but I was happy she told me. After that she said, "And now you are doing exactly what you promised!" I could tell by her voice that she was choked up while she was telling me that.

Before I left Romania, I told my grandmother what my plan was. She knew how determined I was to leave, but she still tried to talk me out of it.

Last time I saw my grandmother was when we went to her doctor's appointment in downtown Bucharest. After the appointment, out on the street I kissed her goodbye. She looked very sad. I could read in her eyes what she was thinking: "This is the last time we will ever see each other."

What happened next is something I believe many people experience as well. We walked away from each other in opposite directions and at one point we both stopped and looked back at the same time. There were tears rolling down our faces. It was very emotional for both of us. She was right; we never saw each other again.

After a few years, my cousin called to tell me my grandmother had passed away. I was devastated and I cried every day for a long time. One night my grandmother came into my dream and told me to stop crying as she was in a good place and she was OK. It felt so real. It was like she was right there next to me. It felt so good to be with Grandma again. The next day I stopped crying.

I am spiritual and I do believe in God but I was never sure what to believe about dreams. Since my grandmother came from the other side to me, I started to believe in the power of dreams and their meaning.

Since that time, I have had a few similar experiences. Recently, my husband Arek had a dream about his family back home in Poland; in the dream the family was having a gathering and were very sad. In the morning he told me about it. That afternoon, we received a phone call from his sister to say that a close family member had passed away.

2018 was a very sad year for me and my family, as I lost my daughter Susie suddenly and unexpectedly. The sadness of 2018 was offset by the joy and happiness of welcoming my fifth grand-daughter Serenna in 2019, and by my love for all of my grandchildren.

My daughter Athena strongly believes that Serenna is a gift from Susie. Not only was Serenna conceived on the same day that Susie died, but the ultrasound technician who calculated that conception date was named Susan. Also, when Serenna was born, we were amazed to see that she had a beauty mark on her nose – just like Susie had.

Pictures of my grandchildren

Pictures of my granddaughter

Me & Arek

As I get older, I value my family and close friends more and more. I like to travel and be surrounded by happy, positive people. I feel that my love of travelling, and my positive mindset, are both useful, as they help me get through the hard times. Everyone deals differently with the loss of their loved ones.

My dear Sue will never be forgotten. Not one single day goes by that I don't think of her and talk to her. The pain will never go away but I am again learning to live my life with peace and acceptance.

For those who go through this terrible pain, I would say to you: please find something that soothes you, as I have with my grandchildren and my hobbies.

My journey has been a very tough one, but I am grateful for my life in Canada, for Arek, and for my family. I am looking towards the future now with love and hope in my heart.

In memory of Susie, who will forever be in my heart.

My girls Athena, Jennifer & Susie.

EPILOGUE

1989 marked the end of communism in Romania and Eastern Europe. Its people can now travel and shop freely. But prices are high and most people are struggling financially. Sadly, some of the people who used to be in the communist party had stuffed money "under the "mattress" and once the country became free of communism, they were able to pull out their money and open businesses. As a consequence, they are still the ones who are enjoying a better life than the average person.

I do occasionally miss Romania, despite my memories of oppression and hardship. It is a beautiful country and of-course I have some happy memories from my life there. Although I would not say I am homesick, I do miss my childhood friends and my cousin Cristina, Aunt Petra's daughter.

I retain a few Romanian traditions; it is in my blood. I still cook some Romania dishes, and my daughter Jennifer does as well. But I am grateful that I made my life in Canada, where I have always felt welcomed, and where I have always been free.

Me and mom

Printed in the United States
by Baker & Taylor Publisher Services